Zoo Animals

ELEPHANTS AT THE ZOO

By Finn Ward

Gareth Stevens Publishing

Please visit our website, www.garethstevens.com. For a free color catalog of all our high-quality books, call toll free 1-800-542-2595 or fax 1-877-542-2596.

Library of Congress Cataloging-in-Publication Data

Ward, Finn.
Elephants at the zoo / Finn Ward.
pages cm. — (Zoo animals)
Includes index.
ISBN 978-1-4824-2589-5 (pbk.)
ISBN 978-1-4824-2590-1 (6 pack)
ISBN 978-1-4824-2591-8 (library binding)
1. Elephants—Juvenile literature. 2. Zoo animals—Juvenile literature. I. Title.
QL737.P98W367 2016
599.67—dc23

2015002594

First Edition

Published in 2016 by
Gareth Stevens Publishing
111 East 14th Street, Suite 349
New York, NY 10003

Editor: Ryan Nagelhout
Designer: Katelyn E. Reynolds

Photo credits: Cover, p. 1 Erika Kusuma Wardani/Shutterstock.com; p. 5 My Life Graphic/Shutterstock.com; p. 7 Pecold/Shutterstock.com; p. 9 Mavadee/Shutterstock.com; pp. 11, 24 (ears) canoni-off/Shutterstock.com; p. 13 TJUKTJUK/Shutterstock.com; p. 15 Aleksandra Duda/Shutterstock.com; pp. 17, 24 (zookeeper) ANGELIKA WARMUTH/AFP/Getty Images; p. 19 Blanscape/Shutterstock.com; p. 21 Andrea Izzotti/Shutterstock.com; p. 23 anyaivanova/Shutterstock.com.

Printed in the United States of America

CPSIA compliance information: Batch #CS15GS: For further information contact Gareth Stevens, New York, New York a: 1-800-542-2595.

Contents

Many animals live
at the zoo.

Some zoos have elephants!

Elephants are huge!

They have very big ears.

They live in groups.
These are called herds.

They need lots of room to walk.

People care for zoo elephants. These are called zookeepers.

Elephants love to eat!

They like to eat
grass and fruit.

Baby elephants love to play!